SUPERBASE 6
CHERRY POINT

SUPERBASE 6

CHERRY POINT

'Can Do' and Harrier II

Steve Mansfield

It would not have been possible to produce this book without the wholehearted co-operation and assistance of countless Marines and civilian personnel at MCAS Cherry Point. Thanking them all would fill the rest of the volume, but we would like to take this opportunity to acknowledge with gratitude the outstanding contributions of Sgt Lissa Sauvé and Pfc Steve Harpster. Their unfailing good humour, skilful logistical support and enthusiasm for anti-social working hours proved invaluable throughout our stay.

We would also like to thank Nikon (UK) Ltd, and John Pitchforth in particular, for help in loaning equipment. All the photographs in this book were shot with Nikon cameras and lenses.

Published in 1989 by Osprey Publishing Limited
59 Grosvenor Street, London W1X 9DA

British Library Cataloguing in Publication Data
Mansfield, Steve
  Cherry Point.
  1. United States, Marine corps. Military bases. Cherry Point, to 1988
  I. Title
  358.4′17′09756

ISBN 0 85045 895 1

Editor Dennis Baldry
Text Simon Craven
Photography Steve Mansfield
Designed by Paul Kime
Printed in Hong Kong

Front cover When you think of Cherry Point, what else springs to mind but the Harrier? After some pioneering work with the AV-8A version, the Marines are now enthusiastic operators of the McDonnell Douglas AV-8B Harrier II. Thanks largely to the design of its advanced supercritical carbon composite wing, the AV-8B can truck the same warload twice as far as the AV-8A, or double the warload over the same tactical radius. After making a classic decelerating transition from wingborne flight, this AV-8B from the CG 2nd MAW comes to the hover before making a vertical landing

Title pages Two-seat TAV-8B Harrier II conversion trainers of VMAT-203 lined up with canopies open before the day's quota of instructional hops

This AV-8A, the last example of the original Marine Harrier to be seen at Cherry Point, announces the primary purpose of the base to passing traffic on the Interstate 70 highway

Introduction

Marine Corps Air Station (MCAS) Cherry Point is the American home of the amazing AV-8B Harrier, the V/STOL attack aircraft that has rewritten the rules for close air support.

The Harrier is famous for its ability to work from short runways or even just a forest clearing, but in peacetime it is most often seen above the skies of this colossal airfield, where four 8500 foot by 400 foot runways sprawl out to form a giant cross nearly three and a half miles across.

Cherry Point is more than just an airfield: it is the biggest Marine Corps Air Station in existence and one of the largest military establishments in the world. Including dependents, over 61,400 people, 23 per cent of the local population, rely on the base for their livelihoods.

Cherry Point has a major impact on the economy of North Carolina. The salary budget alone for its personnel exceeded $433 million in 1988. It is the largest employer in the state. But in many ways, it resembles a self-contained town, with 88 miles of roadway within its boundaries, its own water and sewage plant, shopping centre, numerous sports facilities, hospital, chapel, library and McDonalds. The total plant value of the base is over $1.5 billion.

Cherry Point plays a vital role in the defence of the nation, and it also acts as a major economic boost to eastern North Carolina. The managerial skills required to run it all so smoothly go far beyond those normally used in military life, yet the base has an enviable record of operational efficiency and is well respected in the local community.

The principal occupant of MCAS Cherry Point is the 2nd Marine Aircraft Wing. Its purpose is clearly defined: to act as the Air Combat Element (ACE) for the 2nd Marine Expeditionary Force.

Many observers find it difficult to understand why the Marine Corps finds it necessary to maintain a complete air force of its own, when the USAF and USN have assets capable of similar tasks. Brigadier General James Mead, CG MCAS Cherry Point, explains:

'The Marine Corps' mission is to come from the sea. We all know how difficult that is, as the British found at Gallipoli. So anyone who is going to dare to try that kind of thing should have a tight team, where every element trains as an integral part of the force. So training has a lot to do with it. But more importantly, when you come from the sea there's a distinct limit on what you can bring with you in the assault phase. In the early stages of a battle you may meet heavy resistance before your heavy artillery and large tanks are ashore. The Marine Corps' heaviest artillery is its air element, dedicated to the support of the ground forces. We train as a team in air/ground logistics.'

Major General Richard Gustafson, CG 2nd MAW: 'As the ACE we offer support to the infantry: close air support, air defence, electronic warfare support and base support. We have around 450 aircraft and 15,000 Marines in the wing: six squadrons of F/A-18 fighters, four tactical AV-8B squadrons and one training squadron, three A-6E and one EA-6B squadron, two of KC-130s, six CH-46E tactical helicopter squadrons, two equipped with the CH-53E and one with the CH-53D. There are also two combined squadrons of Cobra attack helicopters and UH-1 general purpose types, and an OV-10 squadron for forward air control.'

That's a lot of aircraft, but 2nd MAW also incorporates numerous support squadrons of ground equipment. The Marine Wing Support Group, MWSG-27, gives logistical and engineering support, and the Marine Air Control Group, MACG-28, has communications and air intercept control facilities for defence. MACG-28 also includes Hawk and Stinger missile battalions.

It is a formidable arsenal of men and machines with an impressive history of operational excellence. 2nd MAW carried out 83 combat missions in the Pacific theatre of operations during WW2, and since then has been deployed during emergencies in the Lebanon, Cuba, the Dominican Republic and the Middle East. Elements of 2nd MAW were also detached to reinforce other Marine Wings in Vietnam. Today it stands ready for rapid deployment to any part of the world, confident that it has whatever it takes to do the job.

Contents

Right Security at Cherry Point is tight. Armed Marines guard this main gate, and sensitive areas such as the flight line are protected by additional checkpoints complete with tank traps to stop even the most determined intruder

WELCOME ABOARD
MCAS CHERRY POINT, N.C.
TO OBTAIN VISITORS
PASS PRESENT:
1. STATE DRIVERS LICENSE
2. STATE MOTOR VEHICLE REGIST-RATION
3. I.D. CARD IF: MILITARY, DEPENDENT, CIVIL SERVICE

WARNING

THIS AIRCRAFT CONTAINS A CARTRIDGE-
ACTUATED EMERGENCY ESCAPE SYSTEM
EQUIPPED WITH EXPLOSIVE CHARGES.
SEE APPLICABLE MAINTENANCE MANUAL
FOR COMPLETE INSTRUCTIONS

AV-8B Harrier II

Far left The transition to hovering flight complete, this AV-8B is seconds away from touchdown on one of Cherry Point's dedicated VTOL pads. Clearly visible are the long under-fuselage strakes which improve the hovering performance of the B-model Harrier by limiting the amount of hot exhaust gases allowed to recirculate into the engine intakes at low speed

Left Lieutenant 'Scorch' Hobauch taxis in. Marine Air has now universally adopted low-visibility 'no-seeum' markings, robbing modern machines of the heraldic colours worn by previous generations of US military aircraft

Overleaf Even sitting idly on the ramp, the AV-8B appears hunched ready to spring into action. This new version of the Harrier sports a retractable air refuelling probe, reducing drag compared to the fixed bolt-on appendage worn by the early A and C models

9

The 000 serial indicates the boss man's aircraft, in this case the Harrier assigned to CG 2nd MAW, Major General Richard A Gustafson. He is an enthusiastic advocate of the AV-8 programme. 'The Harrier is by far my favourite type of aircraft, both from the pilot's viewpoint and that of the MAW commander. After 750 hours flying time in the old AV-8A, I checked out recently on the AV-8B which is a greatly improved machine. Besides carrying more weapons and being more accurate, it's a much more reliable airplane'

Left The gleaming compressor stage of the Harrier's Rolls-Royce Pegasus turbofan can be seen easily through either of the elephant's ear intakes. Engine updates are in progress to give an extra 3000 lb of hovering capacity, giving AV-8B pilots greater operational flexibility in high ambient temperatures, which prevail in the North Carolina summer

Below At very low airspeeds the Harrier intakes lose the ram effect of air being pushed into the engine. To make up the deficiency, these hinged flaps are sucked open, increasing the intake area

Right The Harrier pilot is usually operating under a high workload, but the more docile handling characteristics of the newer AV-8B let him devote more of his mental capacity to fighting as well as flying. Another step forward for the B model is its enhanced ability to fly in poor weather. This is currently being extended further by the addition of a forward-looking infrared sensor (FLIR) which provides the night-flying pilot with video representation of the terrain ahead, projected on to his HUD. A colour moving map display in the cockpit is linked to inertial navigation. It eliminates the need for handheld maps, and keeps the pilot aware of his position at all times

Main picture The extended tailboom of the Harrier houses compressed-air thruster jets. Fed by high-pressure air bled from the compression stage of the Pegasus, they enable the pilot to control his machine at speeds too low for its conventional aerodynamic controls to take effect. **Inset** The pale horizontal stripe on the fin and other parts of the Harrier is an unpainted area of the high technology composite materials which make up 26 per cent of the aircraft's structure by weight. The strip allows easy checks for deterioration

Shortly after sunrise the Cherry Point flight lines are quiet. The solitary 0A-4M Skyhawk in the foreground looks out of place among MAG-32's rows of Harriers

19

Air Traffic Control

The nine displays in the dimly-lit radar room give Cherry Point's controllers the information they need to co-ordinate hundreds of military air movements with normal civilian traffic. Over 800 flights are handled on an average day—Cherry Point acts as the area centre for civilian as well as military ATC

Mockup LHA deck

The superstructure of the mock LHA deck built for carrier qualification training at MCALF Bogue Field, an auxiliary landing field some twenty miles from Cherry Point. The main runway is marked out as a larger carrier complete with arresting gear for practice by pilots of conventional Marine jets

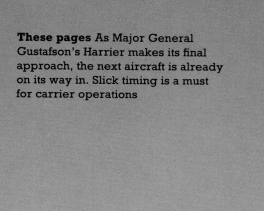

These pages As Major General Gustafson's Harrier makes its final approach, the next aircraft is already on its way in. Slick timing is a must for carrier operations

At the time of writing, Harrier 000 was the only one based at Cherry Point to wear this experimental pale grey colour scheme

27

Although each AV-8B is nominally assigned to one pilot, there is considerable flexibility in day-to-day operations. Here the General's machine is being piloted by Major Steve Patton, a highly experienced test pilot recently based at the Navy's Patuxent River test facility

The darker grey/green colour scheme is the usual choice for any aircraft
expected to hide out in the undergrowth

This page and overleaf Seen from a vantage point on the superstructure of a simulated LHA (landing/helicopter assault) mini-carrier, Flight Lieutenant Tim Cheal makes a copybook approach to the deck, finally rolling forward to clear the landing spot for the next aircraft. Currently flying with the Marine Corps on an exchange scheme, Tim is an RAF officer with several years of Harrier experience

The pilot of the AV-8B has excellent all-round vision provided by the enlarged bubble canopy. Cockpit visibility was poor on many combat jets of the 1960s, but the latest Harrier reflects a determined drive by aircraft designers to rectify the situation

Increased flap area is one of the
features distinguishing the AV-8B
from the A and C

Preceding page and these pages
Although the Harrier is capable of
vertical take-off, it is a rare sight. The
usual mode of operation is STOVL
(short take-off/vertical landing). The
AV-8B can hump a remarkable 130
per cent of its own weight in fuel and
bombs from a 500 yard stretch of
road or runway, though to achieve a
true vertical take-off the load must be
reduced by 9,600 pounds.
Completely redesigned by the
McDonnell Douglas Corporation, the
new-look Harrier uses advanced
lightweight composite materials and
an improved Rolls-Royce Pegasus

engine to pack a much more effective punch. The original AV-8A Harriers promised a little more than they could always deliver. With the best will in the world, there is a limit to how much fuel and ordnance you can haul straight off the ground, and for the AV-8A pilot it was too much of an either/or situation. If the target was just over the next ridge a respectable load could be carried, but especially in hot weather (the Harrier was originally designed for the relative cool of the European theatre) the compromises of range and payload proved too restrictive

TAV-8B
Harrier II

These pages and overleaf Unlike
RAF Harrier trainers, the TAV-8B has
no combat capabilities. The view
from the instructor's raised rear seat
must be the best offered by any two-
seat training aeroplane

Main picture The two-seat TAV-8B Harrier II trainers of VMAT-203 take a brief respite from their duties converting 2nd MAW pilots from conventional trainers or other less demanding aircraft. Note the side-hinged canopies and birdstrike-proof screen between cockpits.
Inset Family group: the TAV-8B shows off its extra length as a single-seater passes by

Harrier maintenance

For engine removal the Harrier pops apart like a model kit. The AV-8B is proving to need much less unscheduled maintenance than the earlier A and C models

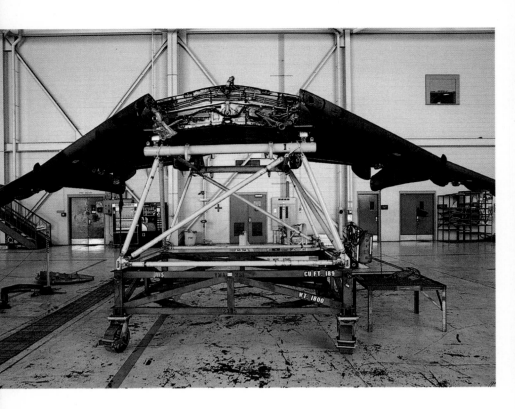

Above The detached wing waits, bat-like, on its trolley for remounting

Harrier 'Hush House'

Right and overleaf Carrying out ground runs on a re-engined Harrier takes a little planning. You can't run it up to full power against the chocks, as it would just climb over. The thunder of prolonged static testing would also disrupt Cherry Point's campaign against unnecessary noise pollution. This hush-house test facility answers both difficulties. The aircraft is literally bolted to the site and advanced acoustic baffling deadens the roar to the point where general airfield noise makes it difficult to tell whether or not a test is in progress

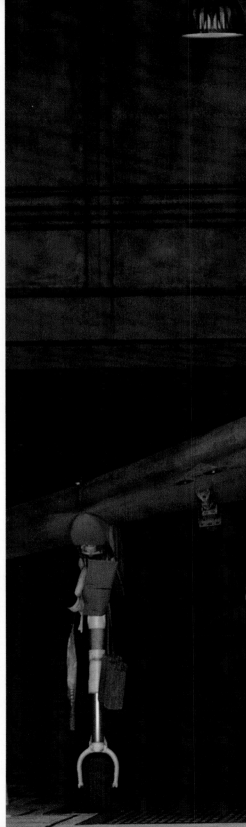

CT-39G
Sabreliner

A welcome flash of glossy paintwork is provided by this non-combatant CT-39G, a variant of the Rockwell Sabreliner executive jet used for VIP transport

UNITED STATES MARINES

A-6E TRAM Intruder

These pages and overleaf The Intruder's reputation is founded not only on its willingness to soak up punishment but also on its surprising airborne agility and an ability to carry practically any load you can bolt to the numerous hard-points. With 28 500 lb bombs bunched like over-ripe bananas under the wings, each A-6E operated out of Cherry Point packs the explosive punch of four of the legendary WW2 B-17 heavy bombers. Actually, this warload is conservative: in wartime emergencies the Intruder has enough power in reserve to cope with considerable overloads. The Intruder clearly shows the genetic rotundity of a true child of the Grumman Iron Works

Previous pages The Wildcat, Hellcat, and Avenger of WW2 vintage were overshadowed in the public gaze by the glamour of sleeker rivals, and the same is true of the portly A-6. But true virtue is more than skin deep. Grumman products may not be pretty, but the pilots who fly them call the factory the Iron Works out of affection and gratitude for the immense strength and dependability of its machines. It also has the invaluable ability to deliver accurate bombing support to Marine ground forces in weather that would keep most military jet pilots on the ground. This is why despite its age (the A-6 originally joined the Marines in 1964), this sturdy machine inspires as much confidence in tactical commanders as it does in its crews

Right Slung under the bulbous nose is the FLIR sensor for low-level flight in bad weather. The Intruder's immense nosewheel assembly is characteristic of the machine's enormous strength. A preflight inspection confirms the impression of massive structural integrity. Everywhere you look there are rivets and bolt-heads, thick flanges and pins, strengthening ribs and brackets, all manner of obscure gadgets sticking out into the breeze

Far right Cherry Point's Intruders are operated by MAG-14. In its twenty-four years with the US Navy and the Marine Corps, the A-6 has served its crews well, but it is an old soldier now. Already the aircraft in service have been re-winged to extend their lives, and under peacetime conditions they are normally now operated with reduced underwing loads to slow the build-up of fatigue stresses. Two-seat variants of the F/A-18 with extensive avionics upgrades are planned as Intruder replacements for the all-weather strike role into the next century

Just like their counterparts on Harriers, A-6 pilots must re-qualify for carrier operations periodically by shooting approaches on to dummy carriers, complete with arresting gear. Here an Intruder successfully completes a dirty-weather approach into MCALF Bogue, near Cherry Point. Unusually for an American combat aircraft, the A-6 has never been offered for sale to foreign governments. When you have a system this capable, it is wise to keep it to yourself

Above Steps for access to the lofty cockpit hinge down from the intake fairings

Right The Intruder is a creature of dark nights and cloudy skies. To fly accurately in low-level high-speed attacks over invisible, hostile territory needs a partnership of two highly skilled crewmembers and some very sophisticated electronics. The cockpit is dominated by the two displays which make it all possible. The BN (bomber/navigator) stares intently into the console of his IBM AN/ASQ-133 computer, plotting courses and interpreting the input of the AN/APQ-154 radar. Another piece of near-magic is the FLIR, an infrared display, penetrating the darkness to reveal the terrain ahead. In front of the pilot is the VDI (vertical display indicator) which translates the radar data into a computer-generated version of the world outside. Superimposed are the indicators he needs to dodge the mountains and drop the bombs in the right place

EA-6B Prowler

These pages and overleaf If the A-6 Intruder is undistinguished in appearance, its sister ship the EA-6B Prowler is just plain ugly. Although an evolution of the basic A-6 airframe, so many components have been reworked that fewer than 30 per cent of the aircraft is common to both versions. These visual shortcomings do not deter unfriendly MiG pilots from queuing up to take a look, in the hope of knocking down a fat and valuable target. The Prowler is the aerial equivalent of the CIA, gathering electronic intelligence from the airwaves and doing its best to throw a spanner in the works of hostile air defences

Above The EA-6B carries no weapons of its own, but can be a crucial element in establishing local air superiority. Once a threat is identified the ECMOs can confuse the electronic eyes of hostile forces by engaging one of eight jamming devices in five underslung pods

The Intruder is a complicated aircraft, with a long list of preflight systems checks. The groundcrews wait patiently

The EA-6B has been stretched out to accommodate four crew in a two-by-two arrangement. The aircraft is heavy with its large crew and black boxes and, despite uprated J52 engines, it has to be regarded as a bit of a dog compared to a clean A-6. The opposition knows that losing a Prowler can really mess up a Marine Air operation, so it is a keenly-sought target, but with a low power-to-weight ratio it can't easily run away from enemy fighters once they have made visual contact, nor can it protect itself with defensive fire

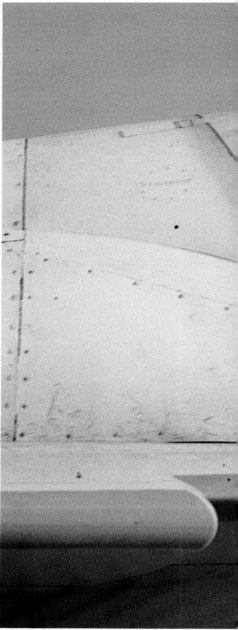

The three ECMOs (Electronic Counter Measures Officers) are the ones who really run the show. They scan the signals sucked in by multiple antennae in the protruberant fin pod and deduce the positions of enemy radar, SAM, AA and fighter assets to create an up-to-date intelligence picture of the tactical situation

The folding wing mechanism is essential to carrier operations using an aircraft the size of the Prowler. Ready to fly, its wingspan is almost twice that of a Harrier

The EA-6B pilot relies on the weather and the skill of the ECMOs to maintain a cloak of invisibility. If that fails—maybe because the opposition has come up with a new kind of electronic magic—a friendly fighter is the only protection. It's a peculiarly stressful feeling for the pilot, having to rely almost entirely on the actions of others for his survival over the battleground. Even at the end of the mission the Prowler pilot has his hands full. An A-6 bomber comes back to the airfield or carrier as a light, agile machine, having deposited several tons of hardware over the target, but the EA-6B still has four men and a full complement of equipment aboard. A bad-weather approach after the stress of a long combat mission is no picnic in this heavily-loaded bird

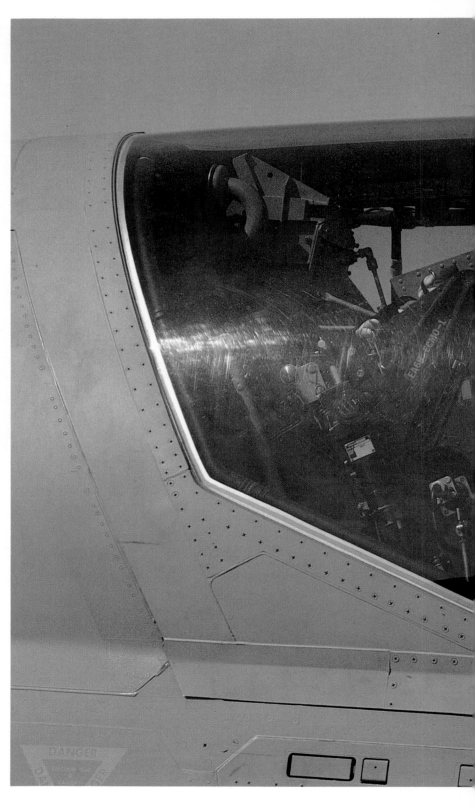

KC-130F
Hercules

Below The cut-out profile of 'Fat Albert' adorns the entrance to the headquarters of VMGR-252, one of Cherry Point's KC-130 in-flight refuelling squadrons

Left The two Hercules squadrons at Cherry Point fly the KC-130 in-flight refuelling variants, though they can quickly be stripped of their big fuselage fuel tanks to perform conventional transport duties

Above The drogue at the end of the
refuelling hose is available in two
sizes, to stream the hose at the right
angle at the different speeds
required by fast jet customers and
lumbering CH-53E tactical transport
helicopters

Right and inset Most large
transports make the crew peer out at
the world through letter-box slits, but
the nose of the Hercules is
generously glazed to give an
outstanding field of vision. However,
the large expanse of Perspex can be
a two-edged sword. In low-level,
high-speed flight, stray birds have
been known to cannon through the
windscreen

Each underwing pod carries a hose reel, here being wound out in preparation for a thirsty F/A-18

Although no F/A-18 squadrons are permanently based at Cherry Point, the type is frequently seen on the airfield. 2nd MAW keeps its Hornets at nearby MCAS Beaufort in South Carolina, where they operate as part of MAG-32, the same Marine Aircraft Group responsible for Harrier operations at Cherry Point. The Hornets are frequent customers for Cherry Point's KC-130 flying gas stations

Far left The KC-130F carries its donor fuel supply in a quick-release tank inside the fuselage. Surprisingly, smoking is permitted during flight in this configuration. A tanker crew spends a lot of time floating around the sky waiting for trade, and any way of relieving the boredom is welcome

Left Maintenance crewman silhouetted against KC-130 fin highlights the size of this versatile hold-all

Search and Rescue

The winchman's view of the CH-46E, just before he is lowered into the sea to pull out a grateful client.

Right and overleaf Four is the normal complement of personnel for a SAR flight: two pilots up front and two unfortunates who flip a coin for the privilege of getting their feet wet. An internal fuel tank blocks the view through the ramp opening at the rear

Above Rescue equipment is packed into internal nooks and crannies. As well as plucking unlucky Marines out of the briny, SAR plays a co-operative role with the Coastguard and often helps civilians out of difficulties

Overleaf The search and rescue helicopter is one of the fighter pilot's best friends. At Cherry Point the SAR mission is carried out by the CH-46E Sea Knight, a Boeing twin-rotor machine of 25 years' service in the Marine Corps

Crash Fire and Rescue

Above Crash and Fire Rescue is a dangerous task even at a civilian airfield, but pulling the occupants from a blazing warplane is truly hazardous. As well as the risk of exploding fuel there is an additional threat potential from bombs, flares and ammunition, and even an intended life-saver like the ejection seat can kill if it goes off during a rescue attempt

Left This Douglas C-118 transport appears intact, but its flying days are over. CFR crews use it to practise emergency evacuations from large aircraft

Above To help them press close to the intense heat of a fuel conflagration, the crews wear visors coated with a transparently thin layer of pure gold, which reflects a high percentage of heat radiation. Each fire truck holds 1000 gallons of water and 500 lb of Halon dry extinguishant on board

Right Getting to the site of a crash is quite a task when the airfield is the size of Cherry Point. The ten crash trucks on site are the massive Oshkosh P-19A, a four-wheel-drive go-anywhere monster that can conquer just about any kind of terrain, even clambering over 18-inch walls

These pages Outside the CFR building, derelict aircraft hulks of all shapes and sizes lie in various states of demolition. Used to brush up on the techniques required to pluck pilots from different types of burning wreck, this forlorn F-4 Phantom bears the marks of sharp axes and power tools

Naval Aviation Depot

Left Other types repaired, modified or remanufactured at Cherry Point include the C-130 Hercules seen here, OV-10 Bronco, CH-46 Sea Knight and of course the AV-8 Harrier. This NADEP also hopes to win the contract for maintenance of the new MV-22 Osprey V/STOL tactical transport aircraft

Below One of Cherry Point's major organisations is NADEP, the Naval Aviation Depot. It exists to perform the most complete maintenance and repair services for Marine and Navy aircraft outside the facilities of the original manufacturers. Six NADEPs operate around the USA, but the Cherry Point establishment is the only one under Marine command

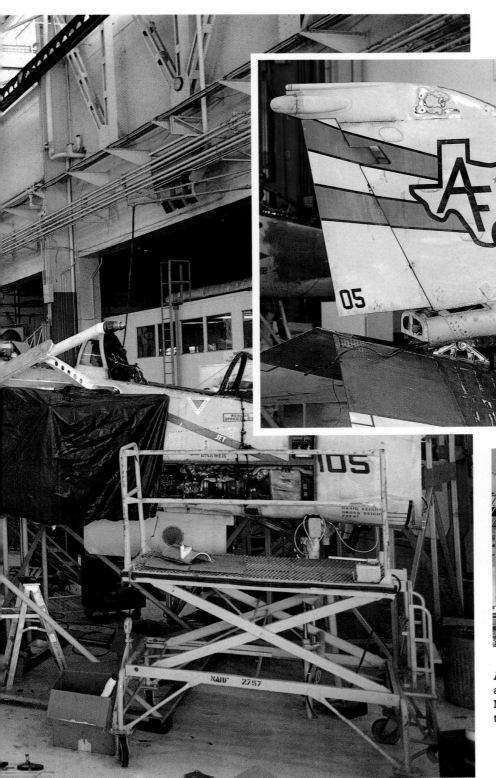

Among the types reconditioned here are the F-4 Phantoms remaining in Marine and US Navy service pending their replacement by F/A-18s

Above Stripped of its paint, this Phantom looks even more weary than it really is. In line with the trend towards greater use of composite materials, this F-4 has been fitted with composite tail surfaces

Right above At the end of a glamorous career as the support ship for the US Navy's Blue Angels formation display team, this C-130 is likely to find itself back in drab operational colours following its remanufacture at NADEP

Right below A reconditioned Phantom is carefully cocooned against the elements until it is recalled to service. The pipe running to the aircraft is connected to a dehumidifier to eliminate any risk of corrosion

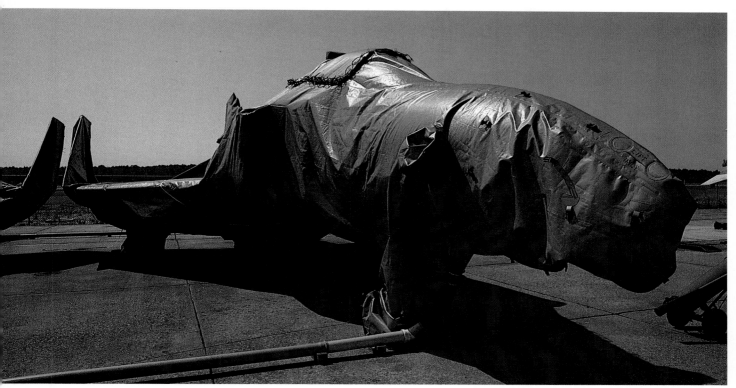

Headquarters and Maintenance Squadron

Left and overleaf MAG-32's Headquarters and Maintenance Squadron runs one of the rarer types at Cherry Point: the two-seat OA-4M Skyhawk. As the O-for-observation prefix suggests, this is a FAC (Forward Air Control) ship, just like the OV-10 Bronco. Its role is to provide a command and communications network linking the grunts with the zoomies, guiding an incoming air strike to where it can do most good. Unlike the turboprop Bronco, however, the Scooter can zip along at over 600 mph, making it ideal for those tricky targets where wide-awake air defences could have an OV-10 for a pre-breakfast snack

Below Sometimes a joke makes a serious point. The Headquarters and Maintenance Squadron (H&MS) attached to MAG-32 performs routine servicing and repair not involving major component reworks or modifications

Above Pulling the whole tail off the A-4 might seem extreme, but it's the only way to remove the J52 powerplant for maintenance or replacement

Marine Air Control Group 28

Right The expeditionary role of Marine Air Control Group 28 includes communications, air traffic control and the protection of Marine assets from enemy air attack

Below Small, light and deadly, the Stinger anti-aircraft missile is a short-range system with high accuracy and a fast response time. This practice system can track an infrared target as small as a matchflame

A mobile Doppler radar system is used to illuminate incoming hostiles for the medium-range Hawk surface-to-air missile battery

Rifle Range

Cook, pilot, driver or administrator, every Marine is a rifleman. Regular re-qualification with the 5.56 mm M-16 rifle keeps everyone in practice. The instructors are distinguished by their campaign hats

Force March

These pages Marines form up for a forced march as a welcome outdoors break from the classroom of their NCO training course. Cherry Point's huge area of 11,717 acres includes large areas of semi-wilderness suitable for exercises

Overleaf Marines get their feet wet. Built on gently-sloping land adjoining an estuary, the base has a high water table. Much of the woodland is marshy and intersected by creeks. **Inset** There's nothing like a few push-ups in the mud to blow out the cobwebs. The stains of the characteristic reddish soil never come out entirely

HMMWV Tactical Vehicle

They call it the Hummer, but its official name is HMMWV, for High Mobility Military Wheeled Vehicle. The replacement for the once-ubiquitous Jeep is a hulking four-wheel-drive monster capable of wading through any depth of water that won't drown the driver. Tall intake and exhaust stacks provide underwater breathing for the engine

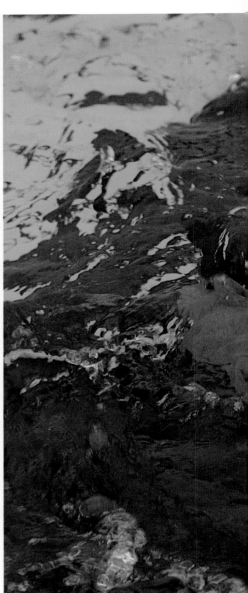

Water Survival Training

Left Sgt Lissa Sauvé looks on as aircrew members suit up for their annual water survival training in Cherry Point's combat pool. The equipment they wear weighs about thirty pounds even when it is dry, so strong swimming abilities are essential

Above The first test is a thirty-yard swim—no mean feat with a heavy weight of wet clothing dragging you into the drink

Next the crews inflate their lifejackets and link together for mutual support

Far left At the deep end of the pool, powerful water jets are mounted beneath a tower. These simulate the tremendous noise and spray caused by a hovering rescue helicopter. A winchman on the tower lowers the hoist to the victim

Left Another test is the parachute drag. Aircrew members are strapped into parachute harnesses linked to an overhead cable. This drags them off a tower and down the pool at high speed. Top marks go to the man who can disconnect himself quickly and safely

127

SUPERBASE
titles in print

SUPERBASE 4
DECI
NATO's European Air Combat Range

Chuck Stewart

SUPERBASE 1
NELLIS
The Home of 'Red Flag'

SUPERBASE 2
MIRAMAR
The Home of 'Top Gun'

SUPERBASE 3
RAMSTEIN
Headquarters of the USAFE

SUPERBASE 5
MILDENHALL
Multi-mission Task Force

Chuck Stewart

David Davies and Mike Vines